Miss Gordon.

Working Life in Britain

1900–1950

Working Life in Britain
1900–1950

Janice Anderson

A Time Warner Book

This first edition published in 2005

Copyright © Omnipress Ltd 2005

ISBN 0-316-73035-1

Produced by Omnipress, Eastbourne

Printed in Singapore

Time Warner Books
An imprint of
Time Warner Book Group UK
Brettenham House
Lancaster Place
London WC2E 7EN

Photo credits: Mary Evans Picture Library, Corbis and
Mirrorpix

Contents

Introduction

The world of working people in Britain at the beginning of the 20th century was so different from our own as to be almost unrecognizable. For the middle-aged among us, the people themselves may not look all that different, allowing for hairstyles and clothing, because they were our grandparents. But the kind of work they did, how long they did it for and what they were paid for doing it have all changed radically.

Before the 20th century, life-long work was essential for the great majority of people of all ages and both sexes in Britain. This began to change from quite early on in the twentieth century so that, by mid-century, the age of the work force had changed at both ends. Children from very poor families were no longer sent out to work almost as soon as they could walk and talk. Now, children of all social classes stayed at school until they were 14, an age that was soon to be raised to 15.

At the other end of the working life, the introduction of old age pensions in 1909 – when they were set at five shillings (25 pence) a week for people over 70 – meant, especially when pensions increased and the age limit was reduced, that a reasonably comfortable retirement was possible for all workers, whatever their social class.

While these changes were closely linked to the growth of the welfare state, allied to the increased political voice won for working people by trade unions, other changes in the world of work in Britain depended much more on what was going on in the rest of the world.

OPPOSITE: *THE WORKING DAY ENDS for men at the engineering and ship-repairing works of R.& H. Green and Silley Weir Limited, still with work to be done in the 1930s* ❧

ABOVE: QUEEN VICTORIA, *Empress of India, gloried in her role as 'Mother' of a multi-ethnic Empire.*

ABOVE: *AMERICAN AUTOMOBILE MANUFACTURER HENRY FORD revolutionized factory production with his car assembly line* ❧

BELOW: *OUT FOR A DRIVE, 1920s*
The Ford Model T car, 'a motor car for the great multitude', was first manufactured in Britain in 1910 and quickly became a best-seller ❧

PAGE 9: *WOMEN AT WORK IN A MUNITIONS FACTORY, c.1916*
Women easily outnumber men in this World War I munitions factory &

BELOW: *UNEMPLOYED MEN QUEUE FOR THE DOLE – unemployment benefit – during the Great Depression*
of the 1930s, when Britain's unemployed reached nearly three million &

In 1900, when the great Queen Victoria, Empress of India, was still on the throne she had occupied since 1837, Britain's Empire seemed still strong and all-powerful, her overseas possessions bringing wealth into the country and providing markets for Britain's great heavy industries. But even as the Empire mourned the death of Queen Victoria in 1901, there were signs that Britain's dominant role in world affairs was almost over. Other countries, especially Germany and the United States, were becoming increasingly prominent in world trade and political affairs and – just as important – in scientific invention and industrial innovation.

By 1952, when Victoria's great great granddaughter, Elizabeth II, became queen, the heavy industries – shipping building, iron and steel production and coal mining – that had sustained the Empire had dwindled to shadows of their former selves and the Empire was in the process of re-inventing itself as a Commonwealth of independent states. In place of those old industries were many new 'light' industries and occupations that were already moving towards the service industry-dominated, car-owning and increasingly affluent consumer society that Britain was to become in the decades ahead.

This book looks at working life in Britain in the first half of the twentieth century from numerous view-points, some of them not directly related to work, but all of them having an influence on how working life changed and developed.

Two great world wars took place in the twentieth century, and Britain was fully engaged in both. World War I decimated a generation of young men and virtually destroyed the old heavy industries and the jobs that they offered. The loss of world markets after the war exacerbated the problems of British industry, so that the 1920s and 1930s were decades of depression, unemployment and strikes, especially in the industrial North.

On the plus side, women, taking over many of the jobs of men at the Front in 1914–18, showed that they had much more to offer the country than domestic servitude. Although they lost most of their war-time jobs when peace came, women over 30 did get the vote in 1918, and women were soon back in the labour market in a much bigger way than before the war. The rise and progress of feminism and its effect on working life in Britain is one of the big themes of this book.

Another is the many changes that have occurred in agriculture, which was in Victorian and Edwardian times still the main employer of unskilled and semi-skilled men. Agricultural workers at the beginning of the 20th century would have had no trouble in understanding the machinery,

BELOW: *THE PRIME MINISTER'S WIFE BOOSTS MORALE, 1943*
Mrs Clementine Churchill, wearing a hat carefully designed to look like a factory worker's headscarf, talks to young rivet heaters and other workers at a Newcastle-upon-Tyne shipyard, vital to the country's survival in World War II

tools and methods their grandparents had used at the beginning of the 19th century. Most of them would have been hard put to know what to do with the tractors, harvesters, milking machines, electrically operated shearing equipment and all the rest that the few of their grandchildren still employed in agriculture used in mid-century.

The rise of the welfare state and the growth of the trade union movement, with the steady improvements in pay and working conditions associated with them, are also important themes here. So, too, is an account of the new employment possibilities, from car-making to film-making, from radio-announcing to gramophone record-production, that enlivened working life in Britain in the first half of the 20th century.

RIGHT: *AIR RAID PROTECTION FOR A BAKER, 1940*
Harold Castell, who had been making bread for 25 years before the war, carries on as usual, his only acknowledgement of Hitler's air raids being to wear a tin hat. Throughout this second great war to involve Britain in the century, workers tried to carry on much as they had always done. Many ingenious ways were found of coping with the results of air raids and getting on with the job ❧

Country Living

LEFT: *TENDING THE FAMILY'S PIGS, 1900*
Pigs were easy to raise and their meat, when salted, kept well and provided the whole family with bacon and ham throughout the winter ❧

OPPOSITE: *A WELCOME BREAK FROM FARM WORK, c.1936*
Farm workers and horses alike look pleased to have a pause for refreshment. The woman, perhaps the wife of one of the men, could be pouring water or cold tea, a favourite labourer's drink, from her jug ❧

BELOW: *THE HAY WAGON, 1920s*
Children help their farmer father bring in the hay. It will be used to feed the horses and other farm animals during the winter ❧

At the beginning of the 20th century daily life in the country did not differ very much from how it had been at the beginning of the 19th century. Although the demands of industry and, from the 1880s, falling markets for British goods abroad, had led to a continuing exodus from the country, the kind of work available to the workers remaining on the land seemed as unchanged as the social background of their lives.

By mid-century, everything had changed. Many traditional forms of husbandry, practised in Britain for centuries before the Romans, had all but disappeared. Horse and oxen-drawn ploughs, harrows and other cultivators, already competing on more forward-looking Victorian farms with steam-powered machinery, had by the reign of George VI, virtually disappeared, replaced by petrol and diesel-driven machines.

At the outset of Edward VII's reign, agriculture had still not recovered from the great depression that began in the 1870s and led

BELOW: *HAND-MILKING AT THE TURN OF THE CENTURY*
These cows have been brought up to the barn to be milked. At this time it was still common to take the pail to the cows, often in the fields – an unhygienic practice to modern minds ❧

RIGHT: *A MILKMAID ON A SUSSEX FARM, 1930s.*
The wooden shoulder yoke the girl uses to carry her heavy pails of milk is very traditional, similar ones having been used for centuries ❧

RIGHT: *MILKING MACHINE IN ACTION*
The milking machine revolutionized dairy farming,
allowing just one or two workers to milk large herds
of cows quickly and efficiently ❦

to a great exodus of workers from farming life. The two million or so people working on the land in 1902 included many in desperate poverty. Only low cottage rents and the produce of the labourers' gardens, which often included keeping a pig in the yard, were all too often all that stood between whole families and real starvation.

Things improved only slowly for agricultural labourers. It was not until the mid-1930s that they were included in the National Insurance scheme and their wages began to climb.

The farms they worked on saw many changes in the first half of the 20th century. Dairy farming changed markedly in a comparatively short time. Cows were milked by hand until the 20th century, and milking was carried out in the field as often as in the barn or farmyard. The milk for the farm's own use, including making butter and cheese, having been set aside, the Edwardian farmer was responsible for getting what was left to the local factory or delivering it to local people. At the factory, it would be turned into cheese and butter, or delivered to nearby villages or towns.

BELOW: *POULTRY FARM ADVERT*
This advertisement for a commercial poultry farm in Mickleover, Derby, was inserted in the 1925 edition of the Derby Street Guide Kelly's Directory ☙

C. R. SALT,

Chestnuts Poultry Farm,

MICKLEOVER.

Send for Illustrated Catalogue
of
Eggs for Hatching, Day Old Chicks,
3 Month Old Pullets, Stock Birds,
Ducklings, Ducks, etc.
Poultry Houses, Chicken Coops,
Incubators, Brooders, Hovers,
Egg & Chick Boxes,
Bees, Bee Hives & Appliances.

ABOVE: *FEEDING THE HENS IN THE YARD*
Many householders with back yards or gardens kept poultry to provide their families with eggs and meat, any surplus being sold to or exchanged with neighbours, and at local markets ☙

The arrival of electricity in the farmyard, at first by way of generators or turbines, allowed dairy workers to use a new invention, the milking machine. The machine meant that large herds of cows could be milked by just a couple of workers. There was no need for a farm worker to load the milk into a cart and take it to the factory, because soon the factory's own milk tanker was being sent out to pick the full milk churns up from the farm gate. Back on the farm, it was unlikely that the farm hands ate much of the wonderful foods made from the milk that they had helped to produce. 'Blown milk' - the thin, blue milk left when all the cream had been separated off - was often the milk they were given to put on their porridge or in their tea.

Dairy farming in Britain got a boost in the 1920s when the government began combating malnutrition among the urban poor by arranging for schools to provide their pupils with fresh milk and low-cost meals.

Much changed, too, in the first half of the century in animal husbandry. Even the humble chicken got the large-scale production treatment from quite early in the century. Although it remained common for farmers' wives to keep poultry for their own use, often selling surplus eggs locally, along with those chickens no longer wanted for egg production, most of the eggs and chickens bought by town and city dwellers came from large-scale poultry farms. Britain was not yet into battery farming, and the birds kept by the large-scale poultry farmers were still kept outdoors or loose in barns or the farmyard.

Until well on into the century, pigs were kept as much by the agricultural worker in his cottage or allotment garden as by the farmer. A good hog, well fed on scraps and properly killed in the autumn, often by a travelling pig-sticker, ensured a whole winter's supply of good meat for a rural family. The head would be boiled for brawn and the rest of the animal salted for hams and sides of bacon. Once they had been properly cured, they were usually hung in the cottage kitchen, covered in muslin to keep flies off them. The meat was cut off the salted joints in chunks, as it was needed. It was a far cry from the neatly sliced rashers

BELOW LEFT: *DIPPING A FARM'S FLOCK OF SHEEP, 1910*
Shepherds and their dogs had to work long hours all year round to get through the many tasks
involved in sheep farming, including tailing, cutting, shearing, lambing, trimming and dipping &

that the town grocer's slicing machine would provide for his customers.

Sheep farming, for both wool and meat, was big business early in the 20th century. Great annual markets like Marlborough Fair would see as many as 20,000 sheep brought in for sale. When a survey of the numbers working in agriculture was carried out early in Edward VII's reign, it showed that, while numbers of general workers had been greatly reduced by the exodus from country to town during the late Victorian agricultural depression, the number of shepherds at work in the country had actually increased.

Like most agricultural workers, shepherds were not well paid and they worked long hours all year round, tending their sheep. Most of the shepherds' tasks – tailing, trimming, lambing, dipping and shearing – were done largely outdoors in the field until well on into the century.

As with milking, electricity made a big difference to one aspect of sheep farming – shearing. By mid-century, most large flocks of sheep, apart from some special breeds on speciality farms or sheep being prepared for showing, were machine-sheared. Large flocks would be brought into the farmyard and penned up before being taken into the shearing shed. Smaller flocks could be sheared in outdoor pens or in the field. Fred Archer, writing about his boyhood on his father's farm in Gloucestershire in the 1920s recalled how his parents would do the shearing together, Mum turning the handle to drive the sheep-shearing machine and Dad handling the clippers.

CLIPPING BY HAND, AN INCREASINGLY RARE SIGHT
Sheep shearing in Scotland around 1940 (left) and in Wales at the end of May in about 1950 (ABOVE). When shearing was done by hand, a rate of eight sheep an hour was considered good going. The arrival of electrically-operated clippers changed all that, but did not change the centuries-old custom of celebrating the end of shearing with the same kind of events that accompanied harvest home an important social event ❧

OPPOSITE: *LIFTING POTATOES*
Horses and a plough help with the potato-lifting at a farm near
Rickmansworth, Hertfordshire in September, 1922 ❧

WORKING THE LAND

Working the land saw such changes in methods and implements that by mid-century the work of farmers and labourers would have looked incomprehensible to their grandparents.

The hand-held scythe that had mowed and harvested since time immemorial was replaced by mechanical reapers, horse-drawn until the 1930s and then tractor-drawn. There were some 40,000 tractors at work on British farms by the end of the 1930s and only the fuel problems of World War II kept horses in use at all. So many working horses had disappeared from the farming scene by the late 1930s that more than a million acres of land, on which fodder for horses had long been produced, were now planted with food crops for Britain's growing population.

Much woodland had also disappeared, so that by about 1920 only six per cent of the once heavily-forested land was covered by woods and forests. Foresters, woodcutters, charcoal-burners and timber hauliers all but disappeared from the country scene. Government action in 1918, when the planting of two million acres of forests was ordered, saved the forestry worker, though his work, wielding a power saw rather than an axe, involved a very different level of activity from that of generations of foresters before him.

A big problem for farmers was the fact that so much of their work, especially on arable farms, was seasonal. Large numbers of workers needed to be hired for relatively short periods, especially at harvest time.

ABOVE: *HARVESTING OATS IN CHESHIRE, 1940s*
Oat stooks, being light, could easily be tossed on to a farm cart, as these women are doing on a farm in the Wirral ❧

BELOW: *MID-CENTURY HAYMAKING, 1950*
A small motor van has become a 'modern' haywain, on to which hay is loaded for transporting out of the field on a farm in the Wirral, Cheshire ❧

ABOVE: *USING A MILL LOADER, 1950*
Mid-century harvesting could involve using an International Cutter attached to a Massey-Ferguson 35 tractor, also fitted with a mill loader, as on this farm ❧

Britain's thirst for beer and appetite for fresh fruit ensured that one county, Kent, had no trouble hiring seasonal labour. Here, a tradition of hiring hop and fruit-pickers from among the workers of London's East End had grown up in mid-Victorian times. Up to the 1950s and 1960s, whole families, from young children to grandparents, would descend on the hop fields of Kent for a late summer working holiday. They earned money and also got good doses of fresh air and sun, even sleeping in haystacks on warm nights.

Elsewhere, many farmers were glad of the fact that school holidays coincided with hay-making and other harvests. Their own children and their friends could easily be found work suitable for their age and strength.

Farmers who specialised in fruit-growing – and there were many of them in Kent and the west of England counties like Gloucestershire and Worcestershire – might need pickers from July right through to Christmas time, depending on the kinds of fruits they grew. Fruit-picking was a time-consuming business because the fruit had to be picked with great care, so that it was not bruised, squashed, or had its bloom rubbed off.

RIGHT: *A FAMILY OF HOP PICKERS, late 1920s*
Three generations of an East End family gather together for a break from picking hops in Kent ❧
PAGE 26: *PICKING FRUIT FOR JAM, 1941*
Jam-making from locally grown fruit was an essential part of the war effort in Britain, and everyone took part in the harvesting. The government rationing scheme made sure there was sufficient sugar to make the jam ❧

The Edwardian Years

Colliery Lasses.

OPPOSITE: *WINGATE MINE DISASTER, 1906*
Local people wait anxiously at the pithead at Wingate Grange mine, County Durham, following an explosion on 14 October that killed 25 miners ❧

BELOW: *BOYS CLEANING COAL, 1910*
Judging by their size, a few of the boys here would be out of work and, hopefully, in school a year after this photograph was taken at a coal mine in Bargoed, near Cardiff. The 1911 Coal Mines Act forbad boys under 12 from working on the surface ❧

In Edwardian Britain, most people, from the very young to the very old, had to work to survive. It was a time when Britain, although still the richest country in the world, could no longer feel secure in her old role as 'workshop of the world', with the world's best markets kept for herself. Britain was becoming a big importer of goods, particularly of food and of coal, which could now be bought more cheaply from abroad than it could be produced at home. All this meant that few workers could feel secure in their jobs.

Workers in the coal industry were particularly hard hit: miners' wages were falling and pits were closing. Strikes were frequent, one of the most serious taking place at Tonypandy in the Rhonda Valley in November 1910. There was rioting, looting, damage to property, and injuries to many miners and policemen.

This strike took place at the end of a decade during which the coal industry, while benefiting from many laws passed to improve wages and working conditions, was still among the most difficult and dangerous in the country. While more laws, such as the Coal Mines Act of 1911, which banned boys under 14 from working

Colliery Lasses.

ABOVE: 'PIT-BROW' GIRLS WORKING ON THE SURFACE OF A WIGAN COAL MINE
The job of pit-brow girls was to screen coal slowly passing on a conveyer belt and sort the coal from the dirt and stones brought to the surface with it. One reason for their name was the bands of flannel they wore round their brows to protect their hair from the coal-dust ✥

below ground and younger than 12 on the surface, were to come, coal mining provided uniquely dangerous work for decades to come.

While strikes among workers in the big industries were increasingly common from the late 19th century, as fledgling trade unions flexed their muscles on behalf of their members, not all was gloom and doom. True, too many people worked long hours for miserable wages, and were ill-housed, poorly clothed and very badly fed. But many more, particularly those not directly involved in the great industries, had regular jobs and were happy in them. For those at the end of their working lives, a major innovation came in January, 1909. People over 70 were now entitled to a state pension. It was not much – a maximum of five shillings (25 pence) a week – and there were many ways in which people could find themselves ineligible for it, but it was a start.

By this time, few very young children were working long hours. They benefited from laws that took them out of the workforce and sent them to school instead. Ways of improving the lot of working women were also being considered. Improvements in the lives of women in the coal industry, for instance, were brought in throughout the period. Women were banned

LEFT: *INSIDE A GROCER'S SHOP, 1911*
John Williams & Sons' well-stocked grocery establishment has its shelves – and the floor – packed with foods from all parts of the Empire and elsewhere. Customers could sit down by the counter while they undertook the lengthy business of placing their orders. They would not have had to carry the groceries home, for the grocer delivered it to the door, either by a boy on a bicycle or, if the order was very large, in a horse-drawn cart – soon to be replaced by a motor van ❧

LEFT: *GIRL WORKING IN A HOSIERY FACTORY*
This 11-year-old girl is earning only a few shillings a week for the long hours she spends making stockings on this large and noisy factory floor. Although Forster's Education Act of 1870 made elementary schooling compulsory between the ages of five and 13, children could take up employment at the age of 10, provided they had reached a certain standard. Mind you the standard was not very high and it is possible that this child couldn't even read or write ☙

from working below ground, but pit-brow girls who worked on the surface screening the coal for stones and dirt, would have to wait until George V's reign to have their jobs 'working on the screens' banned.

For poorly educated women in the Edwardian age, domestic service, followed by work in the textile trades, tailoring and dressmaking, provided the majority with paid work. In 1911, it was estimated that some 39 per cent of all women in paid work were in domestic service.

Tailoring and dressmaking could mean working at home, on a small, 'domestic' sewing machine, for up to 14 hours a day. Women lucky enough to be doing 'better-class' work such as trousers, might earn sixpence an hour.

Just as the invention of the sewing machine gave women the chance to earn a living wage as a dressmaker, so the typewriter completely reshaped the employment of women in industry and commerce. In the Edwardian age more and more of them began to work in commercial offices doing work that

ABOVE: *A WELL-STOCKED FISH SHOP IN HOLLOWAY, LONDON, 1907*
The fish filling the stalls in this shop would all have come through centuries-old Billingsgate Market ❧

had hitherto been done only by men. It is not all that surprising that the women's suffrage movement really got under way in Britain in Edward VII's reign.

For workers not closely tied to British industry or to agriculture, the Edwardian era was a time of comparative peace and stability. In the towns, artisans and the lower middle classes enjoyed price stability, and although wages were low, so, too, were the prices of basic foods.

Keeping the nation fed and clothed was, of course, an essential business. Shops selling food and clothing were the most numerous in villages, towns and cities alike and were major employers of men, women and older children, both as salespeople and as deliverers of goods to customers' homes. Grocers' shops, in particular, were at the heart of the growth of multiple retailing, based on imported goods.

While the Edwardian era may have been a golden age for customers, it was less so for shopkeepers. Edwardian shopkeepers, especially if their shops were of the small, local and cornershop kind, kept them open six days a week, with no early closing on Saturdays – other workers also kept long

ABOVE: *MILK WOMAN IN HER CART, c. 1905*
Milk was often delivered by women. This woman, white apron in place, poses with her equally well turned-out horse and cart for the photographer before setting out on her round. Her milk is kept in metal churns

ABOVE: *A LONDON TAXICAB RANK*
A passenger rests a heavy parcel on the taxi rank, waiting for his cab in Piccadilly. Taxicabs were first legally recognized in London in 1907 and very quickly replaced horse-drawn cabs ❧

hours and needed that late Saturday opening to do their own shopping.

The rapid expansion of the use of motor vehicles gave Edwardian workers a splendid new range of jobs. In 1902 there were only about 700 car and van drivers on Britain's roads. By 1911 there were 48,000.

For all of Britain's workers, whatever the nature of their work, the founding of the Labour Party at a meeting of trade union delegates in 1900 gave a major impetus to the improvement in their working conditions that took place in Edward VII's reign. The rapidly growing importance of the Labour Party, backed by growing trade unions, allied to an increasing awareness among the political classes that working-class poverty affected the whole nation, meant that the Edwardian age saw many moves towards improving the lot of workers.

Steps were taken to cut the worst employment abuses. The wages offered in several low-paid industries, including tailoring and shirt-making, were regulated through Trade Boards, established in 1909, while another act of that year provided for the setting-up of a national network of labour exchanges where unemployed people could look for jobs. The Edwardian age saw the foundations laid for the Welfare State in Britain, with unemployment benefit and moves towards a national insurance scheme just two of the elements that had their beginnings in these last years of peace before World War I changed everything.

LEFT: *FISH BOATS COMING INTO HARBOUR AT STAITHES, 1905*
The day's catch is unloaded from a fishing boat at Staithes, Yorkshire; fishermen bring baskets of fish up the harbour steps, while spectators watch the proceedings ❧

BELOW: *REPAIRING THE FISHING NETS, 1905*
Nets are overhauled and repaired between trips at Scarborough, Yorkshire ❧

SECTION THREE
Working in World War One

LONDON CITY BANK

THE **BANK RATE DOUBLED**

The Globe
CITY SPECIAL

MARTIAL LAW THROUGHOUT GERMANY

WESTMINSTER
LATE EXTRA.

Evening News

STOCK EXCHANGE CLOSED

12 O'CLOCK EDITION

The great war that began in Europe in August 1914 had a profound and lasting effect on all aspects of the way the people of Britain worked. It was the first to be waged as 'total war' – a kind of warfare that demanded the attention of the whole nation, not just of the armed forces and the manufacturers who supplied them. If Britain was to come safely through this war, then industry would have to be mobilized as completely and effectively as the country's armed forces. And it was. The output of Britain's factories changed radically during the war, with munitions manufacture outstripping any other kind.

Unlike World War II, the 1914–18 war was something that, for most people, was carried on 'over there' in France and Belgium, and caused very little damage at home. Fewer than 1,500 people were killed as a result of enemy naval bombardment of coastal towns, or by the few bombs dropped on London from Zeppelins. Factories were not razed, railways and ports were not bombed, or were their workers killed.

Almost from its start in August, 1914, the Great War played havoc with Britain's workforce. A wave of jingoistic patriotism swept the nation, and young men rushed to recruiting offices in their thousands to join up, sure they were volunteering for a war that would be over by Christmas.

OPPOSITE: *NEWSPAPER SELLERS KEEP LONDONERS INFORMED, 1914*
Growing literacy gave newspapers an increasingly important role in British life. As the situation in Europe deteriorated, so everyone relied on newspapers to keep them informed ❧

BELOW: *EAGER VOLUNTEERS OUTSIDE AN ARMY RECRUITING OFFICE, 1914*
The men crowding round the recruiting office at Southwark Town Hall in London thought the war with Germany would be over by Christmas ❧

LEFT: WOMEN TAKE THE PLACE OF MEN, 1917
Women at work in a London engineering factory during the First World War. Women filled many jobs brought into existence by wartime needs. As a result the number of women employed increased from 3,224,600 in July, 1914 to 4,814,600 in January 1918. The greatest increase of women workers was in engineering. Over 700,000 of these women worked in the highly dangerous munitions industry. Industries that had previously excluded women now welcomed them with open arms ❧

Within 18 months, volunteering did not provide the British Army with the huge numbers of fighting men it needed, and conscription was introduced, applying to all men between the ages of 18 and 41. Soon there were no employment exemptions for men under 26; in March 1918, the conscription age was raised to 50. By the time the war ended in November 1918 a third of Britain's working men had been added to the armed forces: in the last full year of the war more than four million men were caught up in it.

As enthusiastically as the men had volunteered for military service, Britain's women volunteered to take their places in factories, shops, offices and on the farm. Many of them left their jobs in domestic service, without regret, where the hours were long, the pay poor and the work little better than drudgery.

When war was declared industry axed many jobs, such as operating sewing and knitting machines in the garment industry, making confectionery and chocolates, and gutting and scaling fish before selling them, that were not considered essential to the war effort. Many of these jobs had traditionally been done by women. The result was that within weeks of the war's outbreak, something like one in seven previously employed women suddenly found themselves without paid jobs. It was some months before the situation was remedied and women began to be given work, including skilled and semi-skilled jobs that men had had a monopoly of before the war.

At first, women were allowed only to fill gaps in 'suitable' trades such as shoe-making, printing and baking. As the labour shortage grew more serious, thousands of women, from as young as 14, found themselves working for up to 12 hours a day and seven days a week for an average wage of 32 shillings (£1.60) in much heavier industrial jobs.

RIGHT: *FULL EMPLOYMENT IN A SHOE FACTORY*
Women fill the work benches in this shoe factory. Trade unions were more reluctant than employers to allow women to do jobs, once the preserve of skilled craftsmen, because it meant a dilution of the principle that only skilled workers should be employed

LEFT: *WOMAN GAUGING SHELLS IN A MUNITIONS FACTORY*
Although munitions factory work was hard, dirty and dangerous, many women welcomed the chance of doing it because it was well paid. For wives and mothers with husbands at the front or killed in action, the extra money was essential, given the very low rate of the separation or widows' allowances ✄

Work in the munitions factories was the most unpleasant, but girls who had previously been kitchen skivvies and parlourmaids jumped at the jobs because the pay was good. It needed to be: women working in munitions factories came to be called 'canaries' because their faces turned yellow from the effects of exposure to TNT and other weapons material.

Munitions factory work was also dangerous, and there were several large explosions causing considerable loss of life during the

RIGHT: *INSIDE THE LINOTYPE MACHINE ROOM AT A PRINTING WORKS, c.1909*
Operating a linotype machine was skilled work, and operators were greatly valued because Britain's increased literacy had created a huge demand for newspapers, periodicals and books. One of the unforeseen results of the government's recruiting drive in 1914 was that thousands of skilled men, such as the ones here, enlisted so quickly that there was no-one available to fill the jobs they left behind them ⁊

war. A huge explosion at the vast Chilwell munitions factory in Nottingham in July 1918, killed 134 workers, most of them women, and seriously injured another 250 of the factory's 10,000 employees.

The war, as well as putting a huge demand on industry, spawned an enormous bureaucracy. Better educated women, especially those trained as shorthand typists, found themselves in great demand in government offices. In London, 'ladies hostels' were set up to house women who had come to London to fill the many clerical vacancies created by the war. In fact, women of all classes found it easier to get clerical and secretarial jobs than jobs in industry, partly because the trade unions were not so concerned about protecting the essential 'skilled' nature of these jobs. By the war's end, there were 50 per cent more women working in so-called white-collar jobs than in industry and agriculture combined.

The many women who returned to life on the farm worked just as long hours as their counterparts in industry and were paid much less. But women on their own could not fill all the jobs on the farm, and the government was very soon looking to other ways of keeping up the agricultural workforce. By March 1915, Education Acts had been put in abeyance in many counties so that farmers and other employers could look to schoolchildren to fill the gaps left by agricultural workers now serving their country in the mud of Flanders. *The Guardian* newspaper, alerting its

RIGHT: *A TYPESETTER OPERATES A LINOTYPE MACHINE*
The linotype machine was patented (by the German-American Ottomar Mergenthaler in 1884) just in time to help in the great expansion of Britain's newspaper publishing industry. The linotype operator's job was physically demanding and, although women took over many of the jobs of enlisted operators during World War I, it remained very much a man's job until the machine was phased out later in the century ❧

LEFT: 'HOLD VERY TIGHT, PLEASE!'
This trainee bus conductor looks as if she enjoys her job on the No.19 bus in London ⁊

BELOW: A YOUNG WOMAN GUARD SIGNALS THE DEPARTURE OF HER TRAIN
This guard on the Metropolitan Railway in London wears a short-skirted uniform similar to that of the first policewomen ⁊

readers to this apparently retrograde step in the care of the nation's children, hoped that ways would be found to ensure that these schoolchildren did not miss out on the education they should be enjoying at their age.

While the numbers of cars produced and driven in Britain during the war declined, partly because petrol became so scarce that it had to be rationed, many more vehicles were needed for war work, not just hauling munitions from the factories but also for many kinds of jobs connected with the armed forces.

Before the war it was almost entirely men who drove trucks, vans and public transport vehicles. Now, women were called into service here too, and more and more women were employed driving everything from buses to milk floats. In 1917, a law was passed permitting women to drive taxis, so women tired of office life in London and other cities could turn to this

LEFT: *ETON BOYS LEND A HAND*
The boys of Eton College can be seen here helping with the war effort during World War I by tending vegetable gardens and allotments ⌘

ABOVE: *WINSTON CHURCHILL VISITS AN ORDANCE FACTORY, 1916*
Winston Churchill, whom Lloyd George was to make Minister of Munitions in 1917, pays a morale-boosting visit to an ordnance factory in Enfield,
London. Both men were keenly aware of the importance of keeping up the morale of workers in this key war-time industry ❧

less confined, more interesting outdoor job instead.

During World War I motor vehicle production came of age as an industry and as an important employer of thousands of men and women. It would help fill the enormous gaps caused by the decline of such great Victorian industries as textiles, iron and steel, shipbuilding and coal mining.

The Great War strengthened the position of organised labour, as represented by the trade unions and the Labour Party. Both were fully involved in the war effort and Labour became increasingly prominent in the machinery of local government, especially in the great industrial cities. Its representatives sat on many public bodies, arbitration tribunals and the like.

As the war entered a third, then a fourth year, and workers became increasingly exhausted and dispirited, the work of those arbitration panels increased too. Men who had for the past two or three years been working seven shifts totalling 90 hours a week, began to show their industrial muscle. From early 1916, strikes became increasingly common among shipyard workers, first on the Clyde, then spreading to Liverpool and the Tyne. Then workers in the major industrial towns – London, Manchester, Sheffield, Coventry – also began to strike, mostly for shorter hours.

LEFT: *TEA FOR THE TROOPS IN THE TRENCHES*
Tea was an essential part of the rations for fighting soldiers. Workers in this London firm are packing hundreds of pounds of tea into tins for sending to the Front

It was clear to everyone that British industry and agriculture needed a new labour policy, one that gave workers and their representatives a real say in the conditions under which they worked and the wages they got for doing it. The man who revived workers' morale and gave the whole nation hope for the future was David Lloyd George, elected Prime Minister at the end of 1916.

Like Winston Churchill during World War II, Lloyd George recognised the importance of boosting the morale of the nation's workers. His many visits to factories, shipyards and coal mines during the war ensured that Britain's workers knew the government was fully aware of their important place in the nation's life.

LEFT: *DELIVERING THE MILK, 1916*
This milkmaid has to push her cart through the town. At least her milk is already packed into glass bottles, unlike that of the Edwardian milkmaid with her churns of milk pictured on page 34 ⚬
BELOW: *CARPENTRY FOR GIRLS*
With so many men at the Front, women had to turn their hand to many jobs new to them ⚬

PAGE 50: *ON AN ASSEMBLY LINE IN A MUNITIONS FACTORY, 1917*
Henry Ford's car assembly line was quickly adopted for other products, including munitions, as in this English factory ⚬

The Changing Role of Women

LEFT: *MRS PANKHURST IN FULL FLOW AT A PUBLIC MEETING*
Mrs Emmeline Pankhurst was a forceful and intrepid campaigner for the vote for women. Her Women's Social and Political Union was the loudest voice in the struggle to gain women their proper place in the political system ❧

RIGHT: *VOTES FOR WOMEN*
Suffragettes, as members of the Women's Social and Political Union were popularly known, carried on an unremitting publicity campaign in their struggle for the vote. Their own newspaper, public meetings, poster campaigns and billboards all played a part in it ❧

Perhaps the most dramatic improvement in Britain's way of life in the 20th century was the change in the place of women in the nation's working life. The foundations for this change, which only reached a climax later in the century, were gradually laid in the decades before World War II.

Even before World War I, when hundreds of thousands of women took over the jobs of men fighting in the trenches, only to lose them within a year of the Armistice, there had been many signs that women would not be willing to remain so totally subservient to men, either in the workplace or in private life.

For women to gain their rightful place as fully equal partners in working life in Britain, two male-dominated organisations had to re-think their attitude to them: Parliament and the organised labour movement, as represented by the Trades Union Congress.

There were politicians and statesmen in Britain in the late Victorian age who believed that women should be given the vote – after all, the former British colony of New Zealand had become the world's first sovereign state to give women the vote in 1893 – but there were few of them.

The women's suffragist movement began in order to get women the vote, which was to be a first step to improving the appalling sweated labour conditions under which so

many women worked. When the much more militant suffragettes of the Women's Social and Political Union got into their stride, they lost sight of the reason for wanting the vote for women, and getting the vote became an end in itself. It has been said that their often violent militancy actually put back for years the chances of women being given the vote.

The Women's Social and Political Union was founded in 1903 by Mrs Emmeline Pankhurst, a long-time member, with her husband, Richard, of the Independent Labour Party. At first, the main aim of her organization was to recruit working-class women into the struggle for the vote, because she thought that having the vote would help improve their often appallingly poverty-stricken lives. Before long, however, she and her daughters, Christabel and Sylvia, were all active – often violently so – in the women's suffrage movement for its one sake and lost sight of their original motivation. Their activities led to their arrest and imprisonment many times.

LEFT: *A PUBLIC VOICE FOR THE WOMEN'S TRADE UNION LEAGUE*
The Women's Trade Union League, founded in 1874 as the Women's Protective and Provident League, was the first general trade union for women. Its aim was the 'formation of protective and benefit societies among women earning their own living' ❧

BELOW AND RIGHT: *FLAPPERS*

Women who had had a taste of freedom and independence during the war did not give them up after it. Within a year of the Armistice, dance clubs and halls were opening throughout the country and young women, wearing shockingly short skirts, sporting bobbed hair and smoking Turkish cigarettes, were dancing tangoes, fox-trots, one-steps and something called the 'Shimmy' to the sound of jazz bands. The Flapper had arrived and would 'Charleston' her way through the 1920s ❧

By the time of her death in 1928, Mrs Pankhurst had turned her energies to the Conservative Party, and was adopted as one of their candidates in London's East End. Only her daughter Sylvia remained active in Labour politics.

When women over 30 were given the right to vote in general elections in 1918 – women over 21 had to wait until 1928, the year of the 'Flapper' vote – it was as much in recognition of the essential role women had played in the workforce during World War I as for the activities of the suffragettes.

The first women's trade unions were formed in the later years of the 19th century. In 1874, Emma Paterson, a bookbinder, organised a general union for women which she and another woman represented at the Trades Union Congress in 1875. Her union, called the Women's Trade Union League from 1891, was influential enough to cause several other women's trade unions to be formed in England and Scotland before the turn of the century.

RIGHT: *FEMALE AMBULANCE DRIVERS*
On the outbreak of the World War I, a lady called Evalina Haverfield supported the decision by Emmeline Pankhurst to help Britain's war effort. In 1914 she founded the Women's Emergency Corps, an organisation which helped organize women to become doctors, nurses, ambulance drivers and motorcycle messengers ❦

RIGHT: *TEATIME SERVICE*
The great British institution of afternoon tea rapidly expanded out of the drawing room and into public tearooms and restaurants in the 1920s. As well as the networks of tearooms that spread throughout the country in the period, department stores, hotels and other public places also had to have large, stylishly decorated tearooms if they wished to attract customers. They also had to have armies of people to serve the teas. Serving lunches and afternoon teas was very much a job for women. The typical waitress's uniform, including a frilly cap and crisp white collar and cuffs on her dress, soon became familiar to people taking tea everywhere from Land's End to John O' Groats ❧

Emma Paterson and her successors had an uphill battle to get the TUC to do more than pay lip service to the value and importance of women's trade unions to the labour movement. Women had long had their own trade societies and associations, covering trades such as tailoring and textile manufacturing, which could be said to be women's work. Many men, however, were actively hostile to the idea of women coming in to what were seen as traditionally men's trades; they thought that the presence of women could mean that wages would be reduced and the emphasis on skills diminished. In 1916, despite the gravity of the war situation and the importance of the docks to the nation's survival, a scheme to allow women to work on the Liverpool docks had to be abandoned because the men refused to work with them, even though they were to work in a separate section of the docks and they would be paid less.

Another reason why the TUC did not have to waste time considering women was that very few women were able to take on the sort of work that was recognised as being worthy of trade union status. In the Edwardian age only about 8 per cent of women with jobs joined trade unions. Until World War I, domestic service was the biggest single source of work for women in Britain. The textiles and clothing industries came next – hence the formation of the Society of Glasgow Tailoresses and similar unions in the 1890s.

Even after World War I, when the numbers of women in work began gradually to rise, the proportion of women

LEFT: *WOMAN PORTER AT THE MAYFAIR HOTEL, LONDON, 1941*
War-time staff problems undoubtedly helped the Mayfair Hotel forget their years-old policy and employ a female porter for the first time in 1941. This woman's smartly tailored uniform looks like a cross between those of a cinema usherette and an American bellhop. She looks happy in her work and seems to have no difficulty in carrying several guests' bags at once ❧

MASS ENTERTAINMENT
New forms of mass entertainment, especially the cinema, radio and gramophone record production, gave women exciting new worlds of work to conquer.
LEFT: *VERA LYNN*
Vera Lynn's uniquely warm and strong singing voice made her hugely popular as a radio star during World War II. Her recordings of such songs as 'We'll Meet Again' and 'The White Cliffs of Dover', sold by Decca in their hundreds of thousands, helped earn her the title 'Forces' Sweetheart'.
RIGHT: *JESSIE MATTHEWS*
Actress Jessie Matthews captured the hearts of the world in her musical comedy performances, on stage, film, radio, and television. Here is a picture from 'Sally Who?' at the Strand Theatre in 1933 ❧

LYONS' OXFORD CORNER HOUSE
Oxford Street & Tottenham Court Road, London, W.1.

LEFT: *OXFORD STREET LYONS CORNER HOUSE, 1931*
This splendid Lyons Corner House, its Union flag fluttering proudly above it, was well sited on the corner of Oxford Street and Tottenham Court Road In London. It was opened in 1923 ✥

LEFT: *LYONS 'NIPPY' CLEARING A TABLE*
To become a nippy – a waitress – in a Lyons Corner House, and wear the stylish J. Lyons and Co. uniform was the ambition of many working-class girls. Nippies were supposed to have got their name because they were nippy on their feet – which they had to be to serve hundreds of customers in an afternoon ✥

in work was kept down by the almost total rejection of the idea that married women should work: their place, unless they were very poor, was in the home, looking after the family. A contributory factor in the gradual rise of working women in the 1920s was the dreadful death rate of World War I, which decimated a generation of young men. This meant that many women were destined to life-long spinsterhood: having a job with a reasonable salary was essential to them.

For the unmarried flappers and bright young things of the 1920s, the working world was a much brighter and more exciting place than it had been for their mothers and even their elder sisters. The growth of light industries and the wide-ranging development of commerce, banking and insurance, and of the catering and entertainment industries, brought about a revolutionary widening of the work horizons for women.

Working class girls with limited education could find all sorts of interesting jobs in the new, airy factories of light industry, and in shops, cinemas and those wonderful new eating places, with their white table linen, shining cutlery and a vase of flowers on every table that Joe Lyons was opening everywhere. It was the dream of many a girl to become a Nippy in a Lyons Corner House, serving excellent food, quickly and cheaply, to thousands of people every day. A really vast Corner House, like the Coventry Street Corner House in London, could employ well over a thousand people, most of them women.

Many women could also work as teachers in elementary schools, which were increasing in numbers and growing in size and as clerks in the Post Office, the civil service or local government, all of which expanded greatly in the 1920s and 1930s.

The so-called 'white-collar' unions that grew in size and importance with the shift in British industry from heavy to light, and which included teaching and nursing as well as more commerce-oriented unions, saw a

RIGHT: *SORTING THE POST, 1920*
The growing postal service was an increasingly important source of clerical and administrative 'white-collar' jobs for women from the later 19th century. Women seem to have a monopoly of the letter sorting work in this post office ❧

LEFT: *NANCY ASTOR, MP, CAMPAIGNING IN 1923*
American-born Nancy Astor was the first woman to take a seat in the House of Commons. She succeeded her husband, William Waldorf, 2nd Viscount Astor, as MP for Plymouth in 1919, when the 1st Viscount died and William Waldorf moved to the Lords. She was keenly interested in social affairs, and clearly happy to be amongst children during the 1923 election campaign in Plymouth ❧

great increase in the numbers of women members in the 1920s and 1930s.

Young middle-class women, most of whom had never contemplated any employment more serious than arranging flowers in their mothers' drawing rooms, could now consider leaving home every morning for secretarial and administrative jobs in commerce and the professions. Their access to higher education took them in increasing

RIGHT: *WOMAN'S HOUR ON BBC RADIO, 1946*
Mr Holland Bennett has an interesting group of women to interview for the Woman's Hour *programme on the BBC Home Service. On the left of the photograph is the beautiful and popular film star, Deborah Kerr, and on the right is Miss Margaret Bondfield, Britain's first woman cabinet minister* ❦

numbers into the universities, from where careers in medicine, law, academic life, business and politics were all now possibilities.

The first woman to take her seat in Parliament was Nancy Astor, in 1919, and the country's first woman barrister was Dr Ivy Williams, in 1922. Margaret Bondfield, a founder of the National Federation of Women Workers, became Britain's first woman Cabinet member when she was made Minister of Labour in the Labour Government of 1929.

By mid-century, women's place in the workforce was accepted as normal. They might be paid much less than men they worked beside doing the same job – an inequality that would not be addressed until later in the century – but they were on the way to being recognised as essential to the well-being of the world of work.

RIGHT: *ASTRONOMER ETHEL BELLAMY AT WORK, 1934*
Ethel Bellamy studies a transit for judging time with the sun and stars at the Oxford University Observatory. Working with her uncle, F. A. Bellamy, she was responsible for determining the position of about one million stars. Oxford University awarded her an honorary MA degree for her work ❧

Taking a Break

Every worker needs a break from the toil of the job. The farm worker eating his lunch under a hedge in the field, the construction worker opening his drink flask while sitting astride a steel beam high above a city street, are not shirking work. They are fuelling themselves up for a few more hours of worthwhile work. And so are the workers leaving factory, office and shop behind for a few days at the seaside every summer. Workers living in coal mining villages were perhaps better off than workers in the manufacturing and heavy industries in cities; at least they received regular supplies of coal to keep their house fires and stoves going all year round.

The need for a break, short or long, was something that Britain's Victorian employers failed to recognise. Owners of coal mines and railway company bosses began a tradition of building whole villages to house their workers, but this was less a matter of wanting their workers to be comfortable and have a roof over their heads as of ensuring that there was a readily available workforce close to hand at all times.

LEFT: *WRECKAGE OF ENEMY PLANE*
Two wreckers take their lunch in the cockpit of an enemy plane at a wreckers yard, August 1940 ❧

RIGHT: *HIGH TEA BREAK, c.1910*
Height has no terrors for this workman as he takes a tea break astride a steel beam high above The Strand in London. The building being altered once housed the Morning Post *newspaper* ❧

ABOVE: *A SOCIAL EXPERIMENT IN WORKERS' HOUSING*
Port Sunlight, on Merseyside, was begun in 1888 as an experiment in social housing. An attractive garden village, it was built by William Lever (right), later Lord Leverhulme, for the workers at his Port Sunlight factories ⁊

A more philanthropic, socially experimental approach crept into the business of building workers' housing later in the 19th century. W. H. Lever started the trend with the carefully designed Port Sunlight, built round his soap factory in 1888. Then came other experiments in building economic houses like the chocolate manufacturer George Cadbury's Bourneville in 1893 and Joseph Rowntree's New Earswick, which was begun in 1901. These were experiments in building houses that were cheap enough to make low rentals possible, but which were also well designed with open spaces, naturally aligned rather than grid-like streets and even gardens for the houses.

While Port Sunlight was intended primarily as a company village, offering subsidised homes to

RIGHT: *GREETING THE KING AND QUEEN AT BOURNEVILLE*
Women workers take time off from making chocolate and cocoa at the Cadbury factory at Bourneville to give an enthusiastic welcome to King George and Queen Elizabeth ❧

FAR LEFT: *WILLIAM HESKETH LEVER, 1st VISCOUNT LEVERHULME*
A soap manufacturer whose world-famous products included Sunlight soap, Lord Leverhulme was one of the earliest builders of social housing for workers ❧

William Lever's employees, Bourneville, near Birmingham and New Earswick, near York, were both undertaken first and foremost as experiments in building good quality social housing at a reasonable cost that would allow rents to be realistically in tune with workers' wages. All three villages still exist, although more as suburbs of the large cities they were built near than as separate villages.

From the turn of the century, the call for shorter hours and breaks during the working day came from the workers themselves and from their trade unions. The call was heeded by employers much more quickly after World War I. During the 1920s many of the factories purpose-built to accommodate the modern production methods of the

LEFT: *A BREATH OF FRESH AIR ON THE TOWN*
Workers from a tin factory in Cornwall, take a stroll down the high street in their lunch hour ❧

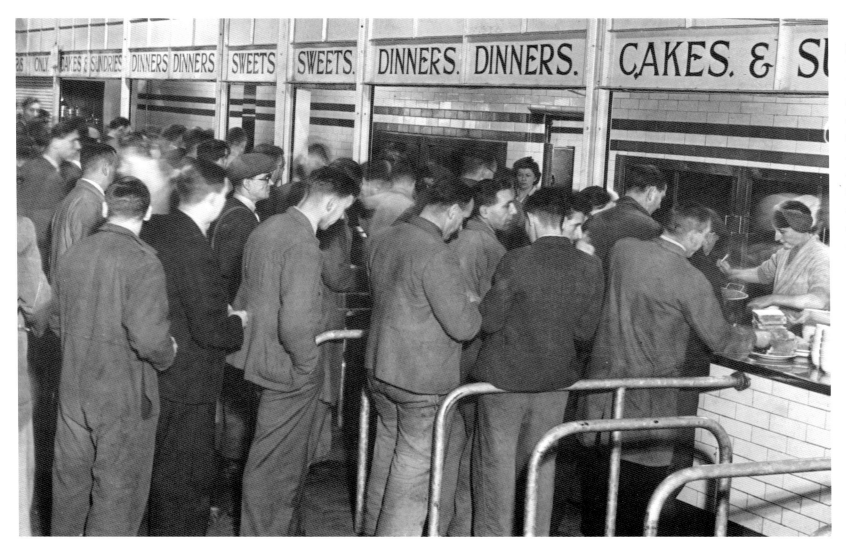

LEFT: *LUNCHTIME AT A WORKS CANTEEN* World War I accelerated the introduction of canteens offering full meals into factories. Munitions manufacturers, in particular, found that well-fed men and women worked much more efficiently than those without proper meals. By 1918, well over a thousand canteens were operating in British factories. The trend was continued after the war, and subsidised canteens became increasingly common. While morning and afternoon tea breaks were often taken round a trolley on the factory floor or in the office corridor, workers queued for lunch in a large canteen ❧

LEFT: *TIME FOR A SMOKE*
It is lunchtime high above London's Berkeley Square and these construction workers are taking time off to smoke cigarettes. The lack of helmets and other safety gear would horrify today's safety and compensation-conscious employers and trade unions alike. The first Workmen's Compensation Act, passed in 1906, offered help for workers, except higher-paid non-manual workers, injured at work, but it was very little, and it was not until much later in the century that stringent legislation covering health and safety at work was brought in. Today, such legislation also bans smoking in large areas of the working environment ☑

new light industries included subsidised canteens on the premises. Here, workers could have short breaks and a midday meal – taking their breaks only when managers permitted. Assembly lines were monotonous, regimented affairs, with overall-clad workers stopping only when a klaxon blared out over the noisy factory floor.

For workers in business and commerce things were rather different. In places like the City of London, the buildings were often old and although they could accommodate the influx of female workers that came after World War I, they rarely ran canteens on site. Through the 1920s and 1930s, crocodiles of clerks, secretaries and other lower-grade office workers, wending their way from their office building to a canteen some blocks away, were common sights in the City.

These lunch places were usually large, plain rooms with long tables set out on a wooden floor and might be used by the staffs of several companies. Once seated, the workers would have food – there was no choice, but at least they did not have to pay for it – set before them. The only real free time these workers had in their lunch hour was the ten minutes 'free time' they had between the end of lunch and

RIGHT: *A LUNCH BREAK IN THE FIELD*
This farm labourer's wife probably made and packed the cheese sandwich he is eating on the job. He may have a flask of tea to help wash it down in his pocket. Workers in agriculture were slow to get the same minimum meal breaks that were enshrined in law for workers in industry ❦

RIGHT: *WAKES WEEK
IN LANCASHIRE
Most people in
Northern England will
have heard of the
Lancashire Wakes
weeks – those occasions
when entire towns
would close down
completely while their
populations migrated
to the seaside. It's
everyday clothes and
no buckets and spades
for the crowds taking a
Wakes Week break at
Blackpool, relaxing in
the sun on the
promenade* &

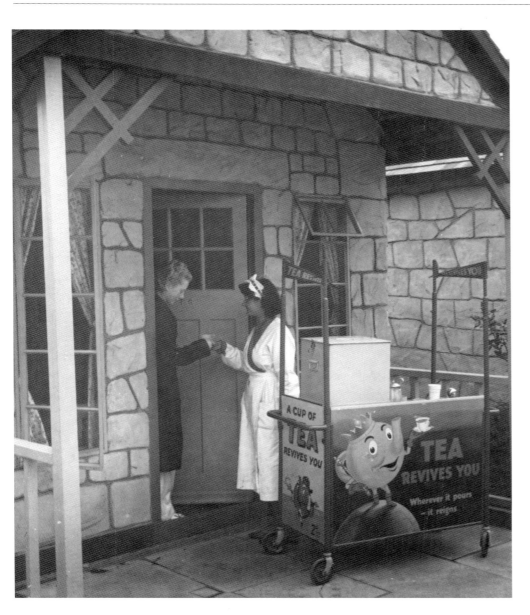

LEFT: *MORNING TEA AT BUTLIN'S*
Early morning tea is delivered to a chalet at a Butlin's Holiday Camp. A ticket for seven such teas cost a bob (one shilling, or 5 new pence)

Below: THE BUTLIN'S HOLIDAY CAMP AT SKEGNESS
Billy Butlin opened his large and glamorous holiday camp at Skegness in 1937

ABOVE: *THE LILO COMPANY'S ANNUAL SUMMER OUTING to the seaside in 1929 naturally involved plenty of the company's famous inflatable boats and rafts being used by workers and their families* ɛ

their unsupervised walk back to the office. Most of the young men would duck into the nearest tobacconist for cigarettes.

The tradition of giving workers much longer breaks from their jobs had two quite different origins. The shorter working week – Saturday after midday and all day Sunday without work – grew out of a mixture of the evangelical Sabbatarianism that made strict observance of the Sabbath day such a gloomy feature of life in Victorian Britain, combined with late-19th-century factory legislation that protected women and young children from exploitation. 'No work on Sundays' was of such importance to trade unions that they were happy to join with strict Christians in opposing any ending of the tradition right up until the 1990s.

Longer breaks often involving holidays away from home also grew out of a Victorian factory tradition. Factory owners in the heavily industrial counties of Yorkshire and Lancashire had, for a long time, given their workers a break at the time of the annual Wakes in autumn as well as the customary days off, Christmas Day and Good Friday. Wakes holidays gave factory owners the opportunity to overhaul and do some maintenance on their steam engines, and they did not have to pay their workers when they were not in the factory.

The 1871 Bank Holidays Act, which added

another four public holidays to Britain's traditional two, Christmas Day and Easter, gave workers more opportunities for having a short holiday. From this time, the British seaside holiday really got into its stride, with thousands of workers and their families, and sometimes whole communities together, pouring onto the steam excursion trains that took them to resorts from Blackpool to Brighton, Scarborough to Skegness.

The slow introduction of holidays with pay gradually increased the numbers of workers taking longer holidays – at least four nights away from home became the official modern definition of a holiday – in the '20s and '30s. By the late '30s about three million workers were given paid holidays. The 1938 Holidays with Pay Act gave another 11 million people paid holidays.

These were the years in which the enterprising Billy Butlin made the holiday camp such a feature of workers' holidays.

RIGHT: *ENJOYING A COUNTY CRICKET MATCH, c.1933*
Knotted handkerchiefs compete with cloth caps and panama hats as the accepted headgear for spectators warding off the sun at this match between Kent and Surrey ☙

LEFT: *A ROOFTOP BREAK WITH A RAILWAY VIEW*
These workers have taken their lunch, including a mug of tea, on to the roof of Paddington Station in London ≋

There were already at least 200 small holiday camps for workers dotted about Britain, but the two that Billy Butlin opened at Skegness in 1937 and Clacton in 1939 took the holiday camp into new, more glamorous and exciting territory.

Back home, attitudes had also been changing in factories and offices. During the 1920s and '30s enlightened employers began to realise that there was more to looking after the interests of their workforces than ensuring that safety conditions in factory or office were adequate. Fresh air and sporting activities outside work hours might be a good thing, too. Among the companies that provided sports facilities for their staff in the 1930s were the car manufacturer Morris of Oxford and the Player's cigarette company in Nottingham. After World War II, many more companies provided sports facilities for their workers. Some of them, such as the Thomas Cook grounds at Ravensbourne in Kent, or the Harrods sports fields on the Thames just out of London, were extensive and well equipped.

The British Workers' Sports Federation was the workers' own answer to the problem of getting exercise outside working hours. Established in the 1920s when the fashion for 'hiking' in the countryside affected men and women of all ages and every class, the Federation's greatest moment came in 1932 when its Manchester committee organised what came to be called the Kinder Trepass.

Planned as an attempt to hike to Kinder Scout in an area of the Derbyshire moors

SPORTS FACILITIES FOR STAFF
Among large companies that provided sports facilities for their employees were Morris of Oxford and Player's in Nottingham. The advertisement for Player's cigarettes (ABOVE) appeared in Punch *in October, 1930. The asdvertisement for the Morris Oxford car (RIGHT), with prices ranging from £285 ex-works, was inserted in the* Illustrated London News *in May, 1939*

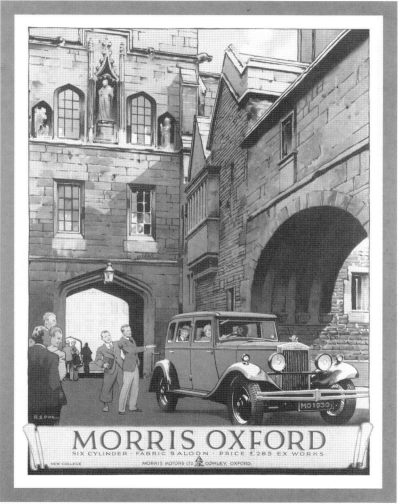

owned by the Duke of Devonshire – and therefore out of bounds to hikers and ramblers – the Kinder Trespass brought 400 mostly young men and women up against the Duke's gamekeepers. During the resulting scuffles, half a dozen young men were arrested and charged with offences ranging from riotous assembly to assault. Five were sent to prison. It was the start of a campaign of demanding access to the countryside for walkers, ramblers and hikers that went on until parliamentary legislation resolved it later in the twentieth century.

LEFT: *BOY SCOUTS ON BEN NEVIS, 1938*
The Boy Scouts movement, which began in 1908 when Robert Baden-Powell set up the first Boy Scout Troop, and its sister organization, the Girl Guides, founded two years later, continues to give many men and women interesting voluntary work as troop leaders outside their normal working hours

Between the Wars

OPPOSITE: *COAL MINING PUTS ITS CASE, 1920*
Londoners read advertisements pasted to a hoarding
putting the coal mine owners' case during a miners'
strike. Miners went on strike for better wages and
better employment conditions in 1920 and 1921 ❧

RIGHT: *CAUTION: DANGEROUS WORK IN*
PROGRESS
Construction workers wear protective masks and
goggles while using a compressed air-powered
concrete gun to spray cement on to a concrete roof ❧

The twenty years between the two World
Wars of the twentieth century was a time
of transition for Britain's economy. The
country's workforce was virtually divided
in two. On the one hand were the millions of
workers whose jobs – and lives – depended on the
country's old heavy industries, most of them in the
north, or on agriculture, which were both now in
serious decline. On the other hand were the workers
who had found jobs in the new light industries,
many of them based in the south of the country, that
were already turning Britain into what would
become, after World War II, a consumer society.

Immediately after World War I, Britain experienced
an economic boom as all the old industries began
gearing up for the brighter future they saw ahead.

LEFT: *SEEKING A JOB AT A LABOUR EXCHANGE, 1920*
For many men disabled in World War I and unable to return to their old jobs, Labour Exchanges were important starting places in the search for a new working life. A network of Labour Exchanges, intended to help unemployed people find jobs, had been set up after the passing of the 1909 Labour Exchanges Act. Quite soon after the early post-Armistice euphoria, Labour Exchanges found their work load doubling and trebling as the 1920s Depression kicked in ❧

RIGHT: *GUARDING THE CHRISTMAS JOINT, 1931*
This butcher in Tottenham, London, has laid in such a large quantity of meat and poultry to satisfy Christmas demand that he cannot close his shop windows. He has called in a bobby from the local police station to guard his holly-decorated stock through the night. This display of plenty emphasises the gap that existed at this time between the relatively prosperous 'new industries' Britain, concentrated in the West Midlands and the South-East, and the Britain of the old heavy industries, most of them in the north, and now in serious decline ⅋

CHRISTMAS 1931
ORDER EARLY FOR XMAS
ORDERS TAKEN FOR CUTS OF

WE ADVISE WHEN ORDERING TO STATE WEIGHT REQUIRED AS
ALL ORDERS WILL BE SPECIALLY CUT!

ALL ORDERS
CARRIED OUT AT LOWEST PRICES.

Although it took some time to get the 4 million men in the armed forces back to Britain and in work, by 1920 most of them had been demobilised and found jobs. Many of these jobs were at the expense of the women who had done them during the war; in fact, within twelve months of the 1918 Armistice, there were fewer women working in Britain's factories than there had been before the war.

All too quickly, that brighter future proved to be a mirage. There were no overseas markets for Britain's old industrial output, especially cotton textiles and iron and steel, while coal mining, the country's largest industry and all of it privately owned, could not produce coal more cheaply than other producers in Europe. Wholesale prices rose sharply while wages either remained static or were cut. Britain's heavy industries experienced a slump that put more than a million people, more than half of them returned servicemen, out of work by 1921. There were strikes and threats of strikes in the docks, shipyards, rail yards and coal mines, most of them for higher wages and shorter hours.

The mass unemployment in the old industries and the near starvation wages and long hours experienced by those still in work found an outlet in May 1926, in the first general strike in Britain's history. The General Strike, made possible by an alliance between the country's three biggest

RIGHT: *STRIKING WORKERS DEMONSTRATE DURING THE GENERAL STRIKE, 1926*
Workers from Britain's industrial heartland bring their case to the capital by way of an organized march to Parliament. The first general strike of workers to take place in Britain achieved little because the Government had seen it coming and made adequate plans to nullify its effect. After just nine days, the Trades Union Congress called off the strike ❧

LEFT: *THE AFTERMATH OF VIOLENT PROTEST, 1926*
This London bus, attacked by striking workers because it was being driven by a strike-breaker, has been abandoned in the street. A strong element of working class versus middle class animosity underlay such attacks. Volunteers who supported the Government by driving buses and trains or organizing feeding stations, were mostly middle-class students or men and women whose jobs were not on the line ❧

unions, those of the miners, the railwaymen and the transport workers, had been threatening for months and the government had plenty of time to work out contingency plans. Supplies were stock-piled and armies of volunteers, most of them middle class and from among university students, kept essential services running. In the event, the strike was called off by the Trades Union Congress after just nine days. For the miners, in particular, the General Strike was a disaster. They held out for six months, until forced back to work – at lower wages – by poverty and near starvation.

The last great effort by working people to get help for the working people of northern Britain came a decade later, and involved the shipbuilding industry. Shipbuilding had been in decline for decades, exacerbated by the depression that hit world trade in the 1920s. At the same time, British trade in iron and steel was losing out to foreign competition, so fewer ships were needed to export its own production. The heroic, despairing Jarrow March of 1936 was the response of Jarrow's men workers to the closure of the town's shipyard and main

LEFT: *THE JARROW MARCHERS ON THEIR WAY SOUTH, 1936*
The march of the unemployed men of Jarrow south to London was non-violent and movingly impressive. But, like the General Strike of a decade before, it achieved little for the shipyard workers whose yard had closed

LEFT: *OPERATING A LACE-MAKING PATTERN MACHINE IN NOTTINGHAM, 1923*
The Industrial Revolution provided the machinery that brought lace-making out of Nottingham lace-makers' houses and into factories. By the 1930s most lace-making in Nottingham had given way to other, more modern, industries ❦

employer in 1934. Nearly 68 per cent of Jarrow's male workers were thrown out of work at the closure. Many of them walked to London, where the Government offered sympathy and free rail travel back to Jarrow, but little else.

While working life in northern Britain was grim to the extreme in the 1920s and for much of the 1930s, away from the old heavy industries, things were very different and even quite prosperous. New, 'clean' industries were growing up further south. Cars, vans and trucks were being built, electrical goods assembled and printing and packaging going on, all in modern factories using new, streamlined production methods. In Nottingham, for instance, the old lace and net-making factories were replaced by factories which were soon to enjoy world renown such as Raleigh (bicycles), Player's (cigarettes) and Boots (pharmaceuticals) emblazoned across their extensive fronts.

The rapidly growing motor vehicle industry provided jobs for thousands of men and women, and not just in

the building and assembling of the cars, vans and trucks. A great network of metalled roads had to be built across the country, there were petrol stations and motor repair garages to be built and manned, and vans and trucks to be driven in a rapidly growing road haulage business. Garages had to be built for the cars that more and more families were able to afford because, as sales of the small cars produced by the British companies Austin and Morris and the American Ford increased, so the prices came down.

Electric power was one of the great between-the-wars growth industries. It required workers to build and man the power stations, construct the networks of powerlines and cables, and to design and make the myriad of products that could use this electric power.

Electricity meant telephones, with many jobs for women as telephone operators before the widespread use of automated exchanges reduced the need for them from the late 1920s. More than this, electricity meant a revolution for heating, lighting and cooking in the home. At the beginning of the 1930s only about a third of houses had electricity; by the end of the decade nearly 70

LEFT: *PRODUCING A WORLD-BEATING BIKE*
The safety bicycle, with its pneumatic rubber tyres,
revolutionised personal transport in the late 19th century.
The Raleigh Cycle Company was established in
Nottingham in the 1890s and grew rapidly. By the 1930s,
its bicycles were being exported all over the world and
the company was a major employer in Nottingham

RIGHT: *BOOTS VAN MAKING A DELIVERY*
Jesse Boot opened his first chemist's shop in Nottingham in 1877. Some 30 years later he headed the largest pharmaceutical retail business in the world. He remained based in Nottingham, where his factories were among the city's largest employers. Since there was a Boots 'pure drugs' store in just about every town in Britain, Sir Jesse Boot (raised to the peerage as the 1st Baron Trent in the last years of his life) was also one of the country's most important employers ⚶

per cent of households had electric light and electric or gas cookers. In the office, electricity powered a major transformation. Open-plan offices now rang to the noise of telephones, tickertape and duplicating machines, as well as to the clatter of typewriters.

There were many new, chemical-based fabrics for clothing that replaced cotton and wool. There was also celluloid which made film, which in turn led to the greatest social revolution of the age, cinema.

The great thing about cinema-going was that it was cheap escapism from daily life. A tanner (sixpence, or 2½ new pence) would buy a good cinema seat, while tuppence would get a place in the 'flea-pit'. Cinemas sprang up in every town, giving work to projectionists, ticket sellers and ushers. The silent cinema also gave work to organists, pianists and musicians, most of whom lost their jobs at the end of the 1920s when

RIGHT: *TALKIES AT THE CINEMA, c.1930*
The advent of talking pictures created an enormous enthusiasm for going to the cinema in Britain. Talkies were so popular that even the great stars of silent movies were forced to turn quickly to making them. The New Park Cinema in Portsea, Hampshire, is showing a pioneering double bill of talking films by two great American stars of the silent era. Ramon Novarro, famous for his playing of the title role in the silent epic, Ben Hur, *appears in* Call of the Flesh *and the great 'Stone Face' comedian Buster Keaton stars in* Forward March ❧

OPPOSITE: *CHARLIE CHAPLIN IN MODERN TIMES*
Charlie Chaplin's 1936 movie, Modern Times, *took a satirical look at the excesses of modern industry. Despite being a silent movie, made several years after almost all other movie-makers began producing 'talkies', Chaplin's film was a great hit with the movie-going public* ❧

talkies came in. While a few cinemas closed with the advent of the talkies, the depression in the business was short-lived. By the end of the 1930s about 40 per cent of adults in Britain went to the cinema at least once a week. Many, especially women, went more often.

Many of those not at the cinema were at home listening to the wireless. The 1920s saw radio arriving in Britain in a big way, with the difficult crystal sets soon giving way to more efficient 'valve' radios, while the introduction of signals and amplifiers meant that batteries with heavy accumulators were no longer needed. A private company called the British Broadcasting Company began making radio broadcasts in 1922. The service became very popular and increasing numbers of people were soon listening to the 'wireless', as it was called, regularly, despite the fact that receiving licences, at 10 shillings (50 pence) each, were not cheap.

The rocketing sales of the broadcasting receiving licences – up from 35,700 in 1922 to more than 2 million in four years – did not go unnoticed by the Government. In 1926, the year in which John Logie Baird first demonstrated television, the company was taken over by a public body with a statutory monopoly on broadcasting in Britain and renamed the British Broadcasting Corporation. By this time it was transmitting 10,000 programmes a year. Most of these were music programmes or talks, but there was also a department devoted to providing a thousand schools with special programmes.

The BBC's growing size and complexity meant that it quickly became one of the country's major employers, offering a dazzlingly wide-ranging list of jobs, from technicians and typists to newsreaders and reporters, from radio actors, dance band leaders and musicians to sports announcers and natural history experts. Years of experimenting with television led to the opening of a high-definition television broadcasting operation at Alexandra Palace in London in 1936 – and, of course, to the creation of thousands more job opportunities in the world's greatest broadcasting company.

ABOVE: *BBC WIRELESS BROADCASTER AT WORK*
Many of the BBC's announcers and broadcasters became well-known personalities, their voices as familiar in households as those of the family itself. This broadcaster, Alvar Liddell, was the man who announced the abdication of King Edward VIII ❧

Work in World War Two

The second great war of the 20th century, which began in September 1939 and ended in mid-1945, was much more a 'total war' for Britain than World War I. In World War II the horrors of warfare did not remain largely outside the country, as they had done in 1914–1918. Within minutes of the Prime Minister, Neville Chamberlain, telling the nation in a radio broadcast that Britain was at war with Germany, the air-raid sirens sounded over London and other cities, providing a reminder that everyone could expect bombs to fall on them any day now.

In the 'total war' situation in Britain, everyone was a combatant. Everyone was involved in some way, either in the war effort, in the business of helping to clear up and keep going after air raids, or in the business of keeping their peacetime job going, whatever the difficulties. Everybody could be killed or wounded in the same way as

RIGHT: *FACTORY WORKERS DEMONSTRATE BOMB SNUFFERS*

Factory workers show how bomb snuffers, a sort of enlarged candle snuffer, work. Theoretically, the holder of the device would place it over a bomb to prevent any fire from it spreading and allow the bomb to burn itself out safely. Practically, the bomb snuffer would have been of little use in a bombing raid ≋

LEFT: *STACKING SHELLS AT A MUNITIONS FACTORY, November, 1939*
Although in the mid-1930s Britain was slow to re-arm despite Germany's obvious militarism, arms and ammunition production was well underway by the time the war began ≋

BELOW LEFT: *USING RATION COUPONS TO BUY BUTTER*
Unlike during World War I, food rationing was introduced early in World War II, with every adult's weekly amounts of the rationed foods being carefully controlled. Everyone had a ration book containing coupons, which were used to obtain the foods ❦

BELOW RIGHT: *CLEARING UP AFTER A NIGHT BOMBING RAID*
Shop girls recover hats from a window display in a fashionable London shop the morning after a German attack ❦

servicemen actually involved in the fighting: nearly 40,000 men, women and children were killed in the Blitz, 20,000 of them in London, and many thousands more were seriously hurt.

The business of clearing up and keeping going affected individual businesses and whole cities alike. Shopkeepers whose shop fronts had been blown out simply put up a notice saying 'More open than usual' and carried on. Bank clerks, struggling into work past bomb sites, might find their banks without electricity or telephones and the glass blown out of the windows. They would clear off the dust, put paper patches over the windows and sit down to hand-write ledger entries and letters that were then delivered by hand, either by the bank staff or by special bands of Post Office workers and volunteers.

RIGHT: *COVENTRY MOPS UP, 1940*
The important industrial city was very severely damaged by a huge bombing raid in November, during which its 15th-century cathedral was destroyed. The city managed to get its key factories back in action within a week &

When Coventry was almost destroyed by bombing on one night in November 1940, workers, firemen and the voluntary organisations managed to get most of the city's key war factories back to full production within five days. There might be tarpaulins over the holes in the roof and no heating except for a few coal braziers, but the workers were back at their machines, working in 12-hour shifts seven days a week.

The war-time government made sure that factory workers, despite their long hours, were at least well fed. From early in the war, it was compulsory for factories to install workers' canteens. By the end of 1944 there were some 30,500 canteens in factories in all parts of the country. Other workers could go to the relatively inexpensive British Restaurants that were opened in towns and cities.

LEFT: *ARP WARDENS AT WORK*
Much of the ARP (Air Raid Precautions) wardens' work involved organizing and mobilizing rescue and clearing-up operations after a bombing raid. The charts on the wall in this ARP station record where all personnel were sent during a raid and its aftermath ⚓

BELOW: *REFRESHING CUPPAS FOR THE HOME GUARD, 1940*
Local women bring tea to members of the Home Guard on patrol at
Christmas time ☙

ABOVE: *CINEMA PROJECTIONIST AT WORK*
Some ten thousand cinema managers and projectionists were recruited into
the Home Guard. One of their jobs was to give troops private showings in
cinemas of secret Army training films ☙

FAR LEFT: *PREPARING FOR THE BLACK-OUT*
The black-out regulations – necessary to prevent enemy bombers being guided by lights to essential installations – were stringently enforced, but did cause many night-time accidents, such as people driving into unnoticed objects like kerbs, lampposts and even walls. These corporation workers in Leicester are painting black and white stripes on roadside lampposts to increase their visibility in the dark ❧

RIGHT: *BUSINESS AS USUAL IN HARRODS' MENSWEAR DEPARTMENT*
The great London department store remained open throughout the war. It had its own large ARP group, recruited from staff, to deal with any bomb damage ❧

RIGHT: *A LAND ARMY GIRL AT WORK*
21-year-old Peggy Ayres, from Watford, home of the giant
Odhams printing works, worked in a print factory before
the war. Now she is a Land Army girl coping well with a
single-furrow plough on a tractor in a muddy, wintertime
field

Many men and women, as well as doing their regular day-time job, volunteered for work in such 'civilian' armies as the AFS (Auxiliary Fire Service), ARP or the Home Guard. 'ARP' stood for Air Raid Precautions, and ARP wardens, who included young men awaiting call-up as well as men past army service age, spent many hours after dark in the early months of the war checking that the Blackout regulations were fully enforced. It was important that no lights were showing that might guide enemy aircraft to centres of population or industry. ARP volunteers were also equipped with items needed to help people during and after an air raid.

Many large organisations had their own ARP groups. The group at Harrods department store in London, for instance, totalled 700 people and included control officers, senior pickets, permanent pickets, wardens, fireguards and the store's firemen, plus members of the Women's Civil Defence Services, auxiliary firemen and special police.

The Home Guard was formed in May 1940 as a defence against the invasion that was expected at any time.

LEFT: *HELPING WITH THE POTATO HARVEST*
Farming was a reserved industry during the war, so important was it for the nation to grow its own food. Many people 'digging for victory' grew food in their own gardens, in allotments in parks and anywhere that a scrap of earth could be turned into a growing medium. They were also ready, like these Hertfordshire schoolchildren, to help with the harvest on farms, where labour was desperately short, despite the recruitment of thousands of women into the Land Army ⤚

WOMEN WORKING FOR VICTORY
LEFT: *Hard at work in a dusty armaments factory* ❧
BELOW: *Inspecting lines of aircraft propellers fresh off the assembly line* ❧

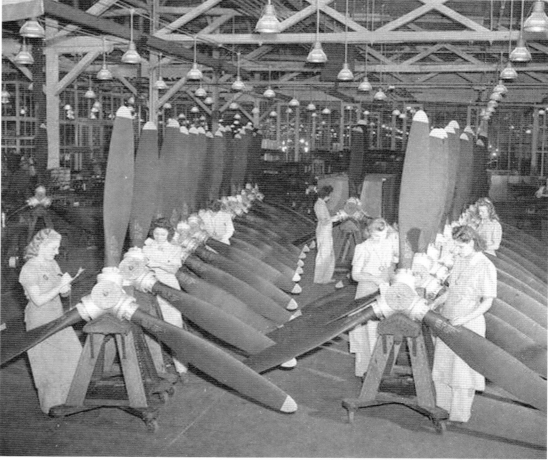

LEFT: *TAKING SUPPLIES INTO THE COOKHOUSE*
These ATS (Auxiliary Territorial Service) members, who are taking care of the cooking at a soldiers' barracks in Lancashire, carry sides of bacon into the kitchen ❧

LEFT: *ANOTHER JOB FOR THE ATS*
These girls look to have enjoyed cleaning the guns they are carrying back to the armoury ❧

Within hours of the announcement that the government wanted to form a force of Local Defence Volunteers, police stations were almost swamped by hundreds of men, many of whom had served in World War I and most of whom were now shopkeepers, butchers, bakers, farmers, bank clerks, or retired, volunteering to join.

The cynical dubbed the Local Defence Volunteers 'Britain's Last Desperate Venture', and when the force was renamed the Home Guard, it was very quickly called 'Dad's Army'. Almost totally without arms or uniforms in its first months, the Home Guard would probably not have stood much of a chance against invading troops. But, once the threat of invasion was past, the men spent the rest of the war doing such essential work as manning anti-aircraft batteries and disposing of unexploded bombs. More than 1200 Home Guards were killed and 550 seriously wounded in the course of their work before the force was disbanded in mid-1944.

While there may not have been the same quantity of enemy action experienced in the countryside as in the cities, agriculture was as much affected by war as were industry and commerce. With Britain effectively blockaded from overseas food markets, it was up to the country's farmers to keep the nation fed. Where the 'Dig for Victory' campaign meant turning city parks into allotments and suburban rose gardens into vegetable patches – even the moat round the Tower of London became a vegetable garden – in the countryside it meant converting millions of acres of grassland and wasteland into land for crops.

With many agricultural workers away in the armed forces, farmers were soon calling desperately for help, and the government turned to women to work on the farms. The Women's Land Army, formed early in the war, was joined with enthusiasm by shop-

RIGHT: *HELPING A WOUNDED DOG*
ARP (Air Raid Precautions) wardens had to deal with so many wounded and lost animals during the Blitz that they formed special Animal Committees to handle them. These ARP women are using a strong box converted into an ambulance to take a wounded Airedale to the nearest animal hospital ❧

girls, hairdressers, secretaries, and waitresses, most of whom had lived all their lives in towns. They worked a 50-hour week, much more at harvest time, and were allowed one, paid week's holiday a year. Their pay was low, the work back-breakingly hard and their billeting arrangements often spartan which was not surprising, given that by the end of the war there were more than 80,000 Land Girls working on the country's farms.

At the start of the war, women had been told the best thing they could do was stay at home or in their regular jobs, but, as in World War I, they were very soon fully involved in the Home Front war effort, working in just about every job that men did except going down coal mines. Late in 1941 the government introduced conscription for women, first calling up unmarried women between the ages of 18 and 30. Within a year or so, about 90 per cent of single women under 40 and 80 per cent of married women the same age were involved in war work of one kind or another. In this war, they were not segregated as they had been in World War I and worked alongside men in many of the civilian jobs they undertook.

Many women found jobs in munitions factories, where the work was difficult and dangerous, but the pay was better than they got

ABOVE: *A BANK WORKER BRINGS A TELEGRAM to Post Office telegraph messengers in the street. For a fee, the messenger will ensure the telegram a quick delivery at a time when bombing raids have damaged electricity cables* ☙

in 'civvie street', or in aircraft factories, where they both serviced and repaired aircraft. They also worked on the railways, both at stations and in workshops, in the Post Office, civil defence, transport and other key occupations.

Large numbers of women chose to get into uniform and joined the women's auxiliary services, where they worked alongside men at home and overseas. There were three services, linked to the three armed forces: the Women's Royal Naval Service (WRNS), the Women's Auxiliary Air Force (WAFF) and the Auxiliary Territorial Service (ATS). Even King George VI's daughter, Princess Elizabeth joined up as soon as she was old enough. She became No. 230873 Second Subaltern Elizabeth Windsor in the ATS.

As in World War I, women did not get equal pay with men, or anything like it, nor did they get any real chance of promotion. What war work did for women was give them the chance to stand on their own feet and demonstrate that, in work terms, they were as capable as men.

The great majority of workers in Britain threw themselves wholeheartedly into the war effort between 1939 and 1945, partly because of the inspirational leadership of the national government led by Prime Minister Winston Churchill, and partly because of the organisations that represented them. The trade unions and the Labour Party either worked closely with the government or were a part of it. World War II helped give the nation's workers a real say in how their working lives would be organised when peace at last returned.

ABOVE: *TRAINING FOR THE FIRE SERVICE*
The AFS (Auxiliary Fire Service) employed men and women in often very dangerous work and so gave them a good training in all aspects of their work. This young woman is being trained as a motorcyclist for the AFS ❧

LEFT: *INSPECTING THE DAMAGE*
The Prime Minister, Winston Churchill, accompanied by the parish priest and local civic dignitaries, sees for himself the damage done to a London church in a bombing raid. Churchill, King George VI and Queen Elizabeth, picked their way through the rubble after many an air raid in London and other cities to show solidarity with the people. When Buckingham Palace was hit for the first time, Queen Elizabeth famously remarked 'Now we can look the East End in the face' ✥

PAGE 112: *CELEBRATING VICTORY IN EUROPE, May, 1945*
Buckingham Palace in London, where the King, Queen and Prime Minister made many appearances on the balcony, was the focus of the celebrations for thousands of people on VE Day, when Germany surrendered unconditionally to the Allies ✥

A Better World Ahead

OPPOSITE: *RETURNING FROM WAR*
Kitbag over his shoulder, a soldier returning from the wars is greeted by his happy wife and son. Their flag-draped home is a 'prefab' (prefabricated), perhaps because their house was destroyed in an air raid ❧

RIGHT: *COUNTING COUPONS OUT OF RATION BOOKS*
This baker's shop in Lambeth, London, has had to take on extra assistants just to deal with the ration books. Food rationing did not finally end in Britain until 1954, nine years after the war was over ❧

Although Britain celebrated the end of World War II with gusto, there was not the same euphoria surrounding the celebrations as there had been in 1918. Then, everyone was sure that Britain was going to be great again. In 1945, everyone knew that the war had cost the country dear, and that it would be some time before prosperity returned. The pessimists thought Britain would never be prosperous again.

At first, the pessimists seemed to be right. The rationing that had kept people fed and healthy during the war was actually extended afterwards, bread being rationed for the first time from June 1946 to July 1948. Rationing did not end

completely until 1954 – a year after the Coronation of Elizabeth II.

But if many foods and other goods were in short supply, work was plentiful. Even for the many women who had to give up their wartime factory jobs to returning servicemen, there was no difficulty in finding a job somewhere else, probably in the newer light industries, in the burgeoning service industries or in commerce, where offices seemed to have a never-ending need for typists and secretaries. Very few women returned to domestic service after World War II.

Returning servicemen were much more quickly given jobs than their fathers had been after World War I. The government divided them into two classes, A and B, and dealt with the B men – tradesmen and craftsmen like plumbers and builders

– immediately. The men were not allowed to buck the system: if a man had been a plumber before the war, then he had to return to civilian life as a plumber. There was certainly plenty of work for tradesmen and builders of all grades in a country where hundreds of thousands of houses had been destroyed or made uninhabitable by enemy action.

Even so, it was no mean achievement that by the end of 1945 some 750,000 servicemen and women were out of uniform and in a job – probably wearing the demob suit or clothing that they were entitled to when they returned to Civvy Street.

Long before the war had ended, the government had calculated that an extra 800,000 workers would be needed to get the post-war economy running again and had put in place many resettlement and training schemes. One of the most effective was a teacher

OPPOSITE: *KEEPING OFFICE HOURS*
Secretarial and clerical work was taken up after the war with enthusiasm by women no longer willing to accept the low pay and long hours of domestic service ❧

RIGHT: *GETTING THE PHONE SERVICE BACK IN ACTION*
Experienced telephone engineers had no trouble getting a job once they were back in Civvy Street. Thousands of miles of telephone cabling and wiring had to be repaired and renewed after the war ❧

training scheme. An intensive training programme was devised that enabled candidates, many of them on army bases, to obtain a teaching diploma in one year, rather than the pre-war two years. Some 45,000 men and women became teachers under the scheme.

For everyone, wage packets were getting fatter, even for women who were as far away as ever from getting equal pay for equal work. Working days were getting shorter, and paid holidays were becoming the norm rather than the exception. Rationing meant that these wages could not be spent on food or clothing, and severe currency restrictions kept people from travelling abroad. The result was that people rediscovered the seaside holiday. In the summer of 1945 Britain's beaches, for five long years hidden behind barbed wire and other anti-invasion precautions, were once again filled with men, women and children enjoying a carefree beach holiday. Their holidays meant jobs for thousands of people, from seaside landladies and beach café owners to sellers of seaside rock and organisers of donkey rides on the sands.

RIGHT: *SELLING OYSTERS ON BLACKPOOL SANDS*
Paddy the oyster-seller would have made few, if any, sales during the war. Now he has plenty of customers for his delicious and cheap shellfish. At this time, oysters were still a favourite working-class food, not the expensive restaurant fare of the few that they became ❧

A seaside holiday was only an annual, two-week matter, but other ways of spending the extra money in the pay packet could be enjoyed all year round. Football and the cinema were among the most popular of the ways in which Britons enjoyed themselves after all the years of austerity and danger.

From the beginning of football's first post-war season in 1945, football grounds saw their stands and terraces packed as hundreds of thousands of people rediscovered the joys of going to a match. More than 85,000 people watched a game between Chelsea and Moscow Dynamo at Stamford Bridge in November 1945. This popularity enabled footballers' wages to increase steadily, so that within decades footballers were amongst the most highly paid young men in the country.

LEFT: *IT LOOKS LIKE A NEAR MISS AT ASTON VILLA*
The terraces at football grounds were packed with enthusiastic supporters in the years after World War II. Television was not yet into its stride and the only way to enjoy a match fully was to go to it, as these fans have done at Aston Villa ❧

Cinema ticket sales soared, too. A survey carried out in 1947 discovered that two out of three young people went to the pictures more than once a week. Cinema's popularity meant that film-making became an important industry, employing hundreds of thousands of people in the British studios, the largest of which were Ealing Studios and the Rank Organisation. Employment opportunities also arose in the cinemas themselves and in numerous side-industries, from publishing fan magazines and film comics to cinema advertising and poster production.

The 1945 General Election that brought the Labour Party to power meant many changes for working people. The new government quickly began turning two of the main planks

RIGHT: *MOVIE-MAKING AT EALING STUDIOS*
Philip Stainton (left) and Richard Hearne (right) struggle for possession of a bike during filming of what was to be one of Ealing Studio's most popular comedies, Passport to Pimlico, *released in 1949. The film was a very funny attack on the regulations, rationing and Whitehall bureaucracy that ordinary people had to contend with in post-war Britain* ❧

RIGHT: *FIGHTING THE 1945 GENERAL ELECTION*
The Prime Minister, Winston Churchill, looks tired as he speaks to voters in the rain at Woodford during the 1945 general election campaign. Mrs Churchill shelters under an umbrella beside him. Churchill retained his Woodford seat, but his Conservative Party lost the election. The new Labour government, led by Clement Attlee, quickly began a major reform of the country's welfare and employment systems ❧

of its election manifesto, the development of the welfare state and the nationalising of key industries, into reality.

Within three years of the election, more than two million workers found themselves working for the state. The government kicked off its programme by nationalising the Bank of England (which was not denationalised until another Labour Government came to power in 1994). In 1947 and 1948 came the nationalisation of the coal mines, which put 700,000 miners in the pay of the National Coal Board, the railways, gas and electricity industries and the long-distance road haulage industry.

RIGHT: *A COLLIERY BRASS BAND IN ACTION, 1946*
The brass band from Penallta Colliery in Wales gives a performance to celebrate the nationalisation of the coal mines and the establishment of the National Coal Board &

BELOW: *THE ALLOY GIRDERS THAT WILL SUPPORT the frame of the Festival of Britain's Dome of Discovery, under construction in 1951* ❧

ABOVE: *THE SKYLON (right) dominated the site of the Festival of Britain on the South Bank of the Thames in 1951* ❧

The raising of the school leaving age from 14 to 15 helped change the age range of the working population. A universal national insurance scheme, to which all workers contributed, provided the working population with a safety net against falling into poverty as a result of accident or illness.

Although the country's economy had still not recovered from the war, by 1951 unemployment remained very low and business was moving ahead in many directions. It seemed fitting, therefore, that Britain should celebrate the centenary of the Great Exhibition of 1851 in some style.

The Festival of Britain, which was opened by King George VI in May 1951, was called 'A tonic for the nation.' A 27-acre bombsite on the south bank of the Thames was transformed into a riverside park filled with pavilions, sculptures, and eating places, all built in striking modern style. The splendid new Festival Hall and a Dome of Discovery dominated the site, and the extraordinary Skylon reached up to the sky in an eye-catching way that would not be bettered until the great wheel of the London Eye was built a few yards upstream to mark the Millennium.

By the time the Festival of Britain closed in September, 1951, 8,500,000 people had enjoyed its attractions and marvelled at the exhibitions of British engineering, science and technology in the pavilions.

RIGHT: *REPLACING THE NATION'S HOUSING STOCK*
Many new materials and construction methods were used in the mighty task of rebuilding Britain's damaged and ageing houses. The machine here, in operation at a plant near Waterloo Bridge in London, was invented to sort and pulverize bomb debris so that it could be made into bricks ❧

The Festival of Britain seemed to point the way to a new, exciting and modern world.

This feeling that a new age was dawning was intensified when King George VI, died in February 1952. Many people wept as they filed past his coffin as it lay in state in Westminster Hall, for he had been a real inspiration and support in the darkest days of the war. But his daughter, Elizabeth, was young and lovely and bore the name of one of England's greatest rulers. The start of her reign seemed to many to be the dawn of a new Elizabethan Age.

RIGHT: *CHILDREN ENGROSSED IN TELEVISION, 1950*
The screen may be very small by present-day standards, but these children are totally absorbed in watching the antics of Andy Pandy, a popular character in the BBC's children's television programmes. Still owned by relatively few, television sets became much more in demand in 1953, because everyone wanted to watch the Coronation of Queen Elizabeth II as it happened and not to have to wait to see it in the cinema – even though the latter showed it in colour

FROM

2'6

LEFT: *TRYING ON SALE HATS*
At only 2/6 (12½ new pence), these hats in C & A's January sale are clearly a bargain. The Oxford Street store, in clearing its winter stock to make way for summer clothes, months before winter is over, is following a trend that would make shopping one of the nation's favourite pastimes. The heavy industrial age had passed and Britain was on the way to becoming a 'consumer society', where service industries employed as large a section of the workforce as the great old industries once had done ❦

RIGHT: *CLEANING WOMEN CASTING THEIR VOTE*
Three Charladies cast their votes early in the morning on February 23, 1950, at the Whitechapel Polling Booth. Labour won the General Election led by Clement Richard Attlee, who stayed in power until October 26, 1951. He will be remembered for presiding over the establishment of the welfare state in Britain and also for the important step of granting independence to India ❧

LEFT: *CHILDREN ENJOY THE FREEDOM OF POST-WAR LONDON*
When winter passes and the summer sun started to dry London's pavements, schoolchildren took it as a signal to appear armed and ready for street games. Pieces of chalk for hop-scotch (left), jackets for goalposts, washing lines for skipping and various other improvisations were produced that provided sport and entertainment after school hours and during the holidays. In the photograph (far left), cockney girls can be seen playing around their council-provided maypole. Often activities are brought to an abrupt ending with the cry of 'Quick, hitch it up, it's a bobby!' ❧